Grace Under Pre

How to Stay Calm and Confident in Difficult Moments

A.T Ramos

Grace Under Pressure

Copyright © [2024] A.T. Ramos.

All rights reserved. This work, including its content, design, and concept, is protected by copyright law. No portion of this publication may be reproduced, shared, or transmitted in any form, whether digitally, mechanically, or otherwise, without the express permission of the author, except for the use of brief excerpts in reviews or educational materials with appropriate credit.

Unauthorized use, duplication, or distribution is strictly prohibited and will be pursued to the fullest extent allowed by law.

AN OUTLINE OF THE BOOK'S STRUCTURE 4

SECTION I: UNDERSTANDING STRESS 7

    WHAT IS MEANT BY PRESSURE? 7

SECTION II: METHODS FOR MAINTAINING COMPOSURE 23

    UNDERSTANDING THE SCIENCE OF BREATHING 23

SECTION III: BUILDING SELF-BELIEF IN DIFFICULT SITUATIONS. 37

    THE ADVANTAGES OF FORWARD PLANNING 37

SECTION IV: DEMONSTRATING EMPATHY DURING STRESS 55

    TYPICAL SITUATIONS THAT INCREASE STRESS 55

CONCLUDING REMARKS: YOUR ROAD TO PERPETUAL CALM 68

    AN OVERVIEW OF KEY METHODS 68

THE END 77

A.T Ramos

An outline of the book's structure

"Grace Under Pressure" is designed to take you step by step through the process of achieving calm and confidence. This book's sections complement one another, providing readers with a full arsenal for overcoming life's problems. As you progress through the chapters, expect the following:

Section I: Understanding Stress

First, consider the concept of pressure in general. You will learn more about the different forms, categories, and effects of pressure, as well as how they affect your life. You'll be able to deal with pressure better if you understand how it affects your body and mind. This foundational understanding serves as the foundation for the practical strategies that follow.

Section II: Methods for Maintaining Composure

Once you've grasped the essence of stress, we'll move on to effective ways for increasing tranquility. This area includes a variety of skills, such as breathing exercises to keep you grounded in the present moment and mindfulness activities to help you focus. You will also learn how to use visualization and affirmations to change your perspective and boost your confidence.

Section III: Building Self-Belief in Difficult Situations.

Confidence is a key component of grace under pressure. This section will discuss emotional intelligence, effective communication tactics, and how to prepare and plan. By refining these abilities, you will be able to handle tough situations with calm, assurance, and empathy.

Section IV: Demonstrating Empathy during Stress

In the final phase, we will bring everything together. You will be given examples from real-life scenarios to help you apply what you have learned. Case studies and success stories will show you how people have dealt with tough situations graciously. We'll also talk about the necessity of establishing a support system and long-term tactics for staying calm.

As we begin this adventure together, I encourage you to read this book with an open mind and a desire to learn more. Being calm under pressure entails more than simply swallowing worry or avoiding unpleasant situations; it also entails confronting life's obstacles head on and demonstrating tenacity. We'll work together to unleash your inner strength, allowing you to thrive rather than simply survive challenging conditions.

Are you willing to change the way you react to pressure? Let's get started immediately.

Section I: Understanding Stress

1. Recognizing Pressure

What Is Meant by Pressure?

The word "pressure" elicits a variety of feelings and mental imagery. It could be your heart racing in an unfamiliar situation, the grip of nerves tightening before a big presentation, or the weight of expectations crushing you. But what exactly do we mean when we discuss pressure?

At its foundation, pressure is the sensation of being pressured into acting in a certain way, typically as a result of demands or expectations from others. It could appear in a multitude of ways, such as deadlines, performance measures, personal goals, and relationships with others. Pressure may help us overcome our comfort zones and achieve our goals, therefore it is not necessarily a bad thing.

However, excessive pressure can cause stress, which is harmful to our health and reduces productivity. Understanding pressure is critical for navigating its intricacies and developing effective management strategies. Recognizing that we are not alone in our challenges might assist to foster a sense of collective resilience, as everyone suffers strain.

Different Types of Pressure

There are many different types of pressure, each with its own set of challenges and complexities. Understanding these categories may help you recognize stressors specific to you and build effective coping techniques.

Personal Influence

The cause of personal pressure is within. It is frequently motivated by our expectations, hopes, and concerns. Perhaps you set lofty goals for yourself, such as sustaining relationships, starting a new profession, or hitting a fitness milestone. If expectations are set too high, the internal pressure may lead to feelings of inadequacy and tiredness rather than inspiration.

Professional Coercion

Deadlines, performance assessments, and job dynamics can all contribute to increased professional pressure, which is typically more evident. The workplace can be stressful, whether it's because of office politics, meeting sales objectives, or managing client expectations. Other signs of this form of stress include coworker rivalry, anxiety of losing one's job, and difficulty managing work and personal life obligations.

Coercion from society

Social pressure stems from our expectations of our friends, family, and society as a whole. This pressure can present itself in a variety of ways, including dealing with family issues and adhering to societal and peer norms. Social media, which we frequently use to compare our lives to beautifully manicured depictions of others, increases social pressure in the digital realm by instilling feelings of inadequacy and anxiety.

Identifying the source of your stress and establishing coping techniques necessitates an understanding of the numerous stresses you face in daily life. Identifying these groups may help you establish a more nuanced coping strategy and a healthier relationship with pressure.

The Physiology Of Stress

To understand how our bodies react to strain, we must first understand the physiology of stress. Stress activates the body's millennia-old "fight or flight" reaction, which functions as a survival mechanism. The release of stress hormones such as cortisol and adrenaline triggers this response.

When these hormones take hold, your body undergoes a variety of physiological changes. This includes:

Elevated Heart Rate: Your heart beats quicker to pump more blood to your muscles and vital organs, readying you for immediate action.

Breathing quickly: You take shallower, more frequent breaths to increase the amount of oxygen in your bloodstream.

Heightened Awareness: This sharpens your senses and makes you more aware of your surroundings, allowing you to respond rapidly to any threats.

These reactions may have short-term benefits, but continuous stress exposure can have a severe impact on health, including immune system damage, heart problems, sorrow, and anxiety. Learning about the physiological roots of stress may help you better understand the need of creating measures to lessen its impacts.

2. Stress's Impact on the Body and Mind

Common Reactions to Pressure:

Understanding how pressure affects us involves knowledge of our normal reactions. While each person's reaction is unique, there are some common trends:

As previously stated, the body's natural reaction to stress is known as the fight-or-flight response. Some people can escape or flee issues (the "flight" response), while others meet them head on (the "fight" response). Knowing your proclivity for a particular response might help you predict and control your behavior in stressful situations.

Physical signs of pressure include stiffness, fatigue, headaches, and stomachaches. These symptoms signal that your body is overly stressed.

Cognitive Overload: When we are under too much stress, our ability to think clearly may be hampered.

Typical effects include decision fatigue, inability to concentrate, and forgetfulness. These mental health concerns can increase stress and exacerbate feelings of inadequacy.

Emotional Reactions: Pressure can elicit a wide range of emotions, including despair, worry, anger, and frustration. Recognizing these emotions is the first step towards understanding how pressure impacts your mental health.

Understanding these frequent reactions is crucial for recognizing stressful circumstances and creating coping strategies. Being conscious of your reactions can allow you to deal with them more effectively, so improving your overall well-being.

Psychological Effects of Stress

Stress can have profound and long-lasting psychological consequences. Extended durations of stress can change brain function, affecting memory, attention, and decision-making. Prolonged exposure to high-pressure environments may result in:

Anxiety disorders are characterized by excessive worry or concern that interferes with daily functioning. Persistent pressure may be a contributing factor to several disorders.

Depression: Severe stress can cause thoughts of hopelessness and worthlessness, as well as a loss of interest in previously enjoyed activities.

Long-term exposure to stress in both personal and professional situations can lead to burnout, a chronic stress syndrome. Its usual symptoms include reduced performance, emotional weariness, and disconnection.

Relationship Implications: Overstress can cause emotional disengagement, increased conflict, and misunderstandings. This loneliness could set off a vicious cycle in which stress exacerbates interpersonal troubles, which exacerbates stress even further.

Building resilience and executing stress management strategies necessitate an awareness of the psychological repercussions of strain. You'll feel more secure asking for help and making constructive adjustments if you understand that these consequences are not personal flaws, but rather common reactions.

Being Aware of Personal Stressors

To manage pressure efficiently, you must first recognize your stressors. A stress trigger is anything that activates your stress reaction and makes you feel uneasy or under pressure. Being aware of your triggers can help you handle stress more effectively.

To identify your stress triggers, consider the following actions:

Maintain a Stress Diary: Keep a journal in which you record stressful experiences. Take notes on the conditions of each incident, as well as your bodily and emotional reactions to it. As patterns emerge over time, it may become evident what your main triggers are.

Think Back to Past Experiences: Remember moments when you felt overwhelmed. What traits did they all share? Were there any individuals, places, or events that consistently generated stress?

Observe Your Body: Pay attention to how your body responds to various events. Your body's responses can give you clues about what causes your stress. Do you feel uncomfortable around specific people or when you have tasks to complete, for example?

Speak with Others: Your loved ones may be able to provide good guidance on the issues that anger you. Check with your close friends and family to see if they have seen any trends in your conduct when you are under strain.

You may be able to mitigate the effects of stress triggers by being proactive and recognizing them. Knowing what triggers you allows you to react deliberately rather than impulsively, whether it involves setting boundaries, adjusting your surroundings, or developing coping strategies.

3. Importance of Mindset

Growth versus. Fixed Mindset.

Our mentality has a significant influence on how we respond to stress and obstacles. Carol Dweck's research on development and fixed mentalities gives light on how our self-perceptions influence how we respond to stressful situations.

Fixed Mindset: People with a fixed mindset feel that their aptitude, intelligence, and talents are constant. They may interpret obstructions as threats and escape potentially difficult situations for fear of failure. This type of thinking may heighten stress and make someone hesitant to venture outside of their comfort zone.

Individuals with a progress attitude, on the other hand, regard problems as chances for learning and personal development. They believe that through patience, time, effort, and courage, they can improve their skills. This point of view encourages curiosity, allowing people to respond to pressure confidently and adaptably.

A development attitude is necessary for becoming resilient in the face of hardship. Individuals with a development attitude are more likely to confront obstacles, accept constructive criticism, and learn from their mistakes. Instead of perceiving failure as a reflection on their personal value, they see it as an opportunity for growth.

Developing a Resilient Mentality

Resilience, or the ability to withstand adversity, is intimately related to our mindset. Developing routines and habits that promote emotional fortitude and flexibility is an essential component of cultivating a resilient mindset. Here are a few techniques to promote resilience:

Accept Challenges: See challenges as opportunities for personal progress rather than hurdles to overcome. Shifting your attitude boosts your willingness to learn and develop.

Practice Self-Compassion: Be gentle to yourself when you face setbacks or hurdles in life. Recognize that everyone has issues, and that if you have self-compassion, you can deal with them effectively.

Set Realistic ambitions: Break down larger ambitions into manageable steps. With this method, you may celebrate little triumphs while gradually increasing your confidence, which helps to reduce the intimidating aspect of larger jobs.

Surround yourself with uplifting, positive people who will encourage and support you. A robust support network can provide critical insight and aid while under stress.

Mindfulness techniques such as meditation or deep breathing can help you stay anchored in the present moment. Mindfulness activities can help you manage stress and build calmness.

Think Back on Your Past Resilience: Remember moments when you overcame adversity. If you can see that you have overcome obstacles in the past, you will feel more confident in your ability to manage current demands.

By implementing these tactics, you may develop a resilient attitude, which will boost your confidence and make it easier to deal with pressure. Resilience is all about learning how to manage stress rather than trying to eradicate it.

The Power of Positive Thinking

Our emotional and physical responses to stress are primarily determined by brain activities. The discipline of positive thinking, which comprises focusing on constructive and uplifting ideas, can significantly improve our ability to manage stress.

Reframe Negative Thoughts: When dealing with stress, it is easy to get into a negative thought cycle. To counter these ideas, restate them in a more constructive or positive light. Instead of saying, "I can't handle this," rephrase it as, "I've faced challenges before, and I can learn to manage this."

Visualize Success: Visualization is an effective approach for increasing confidence and decreasing worry. Spend some time envisioning yourself managing difficult situations with elegance, emphasizing your sense of success and the benefits.

Practice thankfulness: By cultivating thankfulness, you can redirect your focus away from problems and toward the good things in your life. Consider keeping a gratitude diary in which you can list your blessings to help you maintain a cheerful attitude.

Embrace Positive Influences: To surround yourself with positive influences, build a network of people who will support you, watch inspirational videos, and attend motivational talks. Positivity in your environment may help you keep an optimistic attitude.

Practice Positive Affirmations: Telling yourself aloud how talented and skilled you are will make you feel stronger and more confident. Make a list of your favorite affirmations and refer to it often.

You may improve your relationship with pressure by using the power of positive thinking to face challenges front on and take the initiative. Thinking positively includes facing obstacles head on with perseverance and optimism, rather than disregarding them.

Section II: Methods for Maintaining Composure

In a continuously changing environment, understanding how to alleviate stress and maintain inner serenity is critical. This section of the book discusses effective ways to keep your cool. These abilities can help you build resilience and improve your general well-being. Breathing exercises, mindfulness practices, and visualization and affirmation techniques can be combined to create a stress-reduction and wellbeing toolkit.

4. Techniques for Inhalation

Understanding the Science of Breathing

Breathing is not only an automatic function; it also has significant psychological and physiological impacts. Breathing influences the autonomic nervous system, which regulates involuntary body activities such as respiration, digestion, and heart rate. When we are stressed, our bodies frequently go into a fight-or-flight response, which is characterized by rapid, shallow breathing. This response worsens pain and anxiety and causes the release of stress hormones such as cortisol.

However, slow, deep breathing activates the parasympathetic nervous system, which promotes relaxation and reduces stress. Breath control has been demonstrated in trials to lower blood pressure, improve blood pressure regulation, and even boost cognitive performance. Once you understand this technique, you can use your breath to provide quick relief.

Techniques for Instant Peace.

4-7-8 Breathing.

The 4-7-8 breathing method is a simple but efficient way to de-stress quickly. Dr. Andrew Weil created this technique, which promotes deep, rhythmic breathing to achieve calm.

How the 4-7-8 Order is Breathed

Select a Comfortable Position: When sitting or lying down, keep your back straight.

Close your eyes and take some time to unwind in your personal place. Close your eyes and concentrate on your breath.

Inhale: Take four deep, quiet breaths through your nose.

Take a seven-count breathhold.

Exhale: For eight counts, create a whooshing noise and let out all of your breath through your mouth.

Repeat this cycle four times, increasing the number of reps as you feel more comfortable.

This technique may be used anywhere, including your desk, your car, or even a crowded venue, making it ideal for stress management on-the-spot.

Diaphragmatic Breathing.

The goal of diaphragmatic breathing, also known as abdominal or deep breathing, is to improve relaxation and increase oxygen intake by fully contracting the diaphragm.

Guidelines for Diaphragmatic Breathing:

Position: Bend your knees and lie flat on your back, or find a comfortable chair. Hold your chest with one hand and your abdomen in the other.

Inhale deeply via your nose, keeping your chest relatively steady and your abdomen rising. Try to count to four.

Pause: As you hold your breath, notice how full your lungs feel.

Allow your stomach to fall as you exhale gently through your lips. Aim for a count of six to eight.

Repeat this exercise for five to ten minutes, focusing on the rise and fall of your abdomen.

Diaphragmatic breathing can help you relax, reduce anxiety, and breathe more deeply. You may work it into your daily schedule.

Breathing is part of daily activities.

Breathing exercises are simple to include into your daily routine, allowing you to establish a regular practice that promotes relaxation and resilience. Here are a few helpful suggestions:

Make the most of technology by scheduling reminders. Make a mental note to utilize your phone

A.T Ramos

or computer to practice breathing exercises throughout the day.

Create a Ritual: Set aside certain times to do breathing exercises, such as right before bed to encourage undisturbed sleep or first thing in the morning before starting the day.

Mix with Other Activities: For a more relaxing experience, combine breathing techniques with yoga, stretching, and meditation. This combination promotes relaxation and develops a comprehensive stress-reduction strategy.

Practice Mindfully: Pay attention to your breathing throughout the day. When you're walking, eating, or waiting in line, take a moment to notice your breath and let it ground you in the present.

Incorporating breathing exercises into your daily practice can help you develop a calm and present-mindedness that will protect you from stressors.

5. Mindfulness & Meditation

What is mindfulness exactly?

Mindfulness is the practice of remaining fully present and engaged in the present moment, free of distractions and judgment. It entails learning to be mindful of your thoughts, feelings, body, and surroundings. By focusing on the present moment, you can detach from difficult events and improve your ability to control your emotions and remain resilient.

Numerous research have shown that mindfulness improves focus, reduces anxiety, and improves emotional well-being. When you incorporate mindfulness into your everyday practice, you may discover a useful tool for managing stress and achieving inner peace.

Simple Mindfulness Methods

Intentionally inhale: Start with your breath. Close your eyes briefly and concentrate on your inhalations and exhalations. Examine the sensation of the breath entering and exiting your body. When your thoughts wander, gently redirect your attention back to your breathing without passing judgment.

To perform a body scan, close your eyes and sit or lie down. Begin with your toes and mentally scan your body, paying close attention to any tightness, discomfort, or sensations. To relieve stress, breathe deeply through your head, arms, legs, chest, and abdomen.

Choose a modest amount of food, such as a raisin or a piece of fruit, and eat attentively. Take a moment to notice its color, texture, and aroma. Enjoy the eating experience to the fullest by attentively savoring each bite and absorbing the flavors and feelings.

Going on a nature walk allows you to spend time outside and engages your senses. Consider the colors of the foliage, the sounds of the birds, and the sensation of the breeze on your skin. Allow yourself to become fully immersed in the natural environment. Writing in a mindfulness journal: Set aside a specified amount of time each day to objectively record your thoughts and emotions. Consider your past experiences and take note of any instances of thankfulness, stress, or realization.

Including these basic mindfulness techniques in your daily routine will help you become more aware and reduce stress, improving your overall quality of life.

Guided Meditation for Stress Reduction

Guided meditation is one of the most effective ways to relax and refocus your attention. Numerous apps and online programs are available that provide guided meditations for a variety of purposes, such as self-compassion, stress reduction, and falling asleep. Here are some effective ways to incorporate guided meditations into your everyday practice:

Set aside a certain time each day to practice meditation. You might do it in the evening to unwind before bed, or in the morning to start your day off well.

Create a Comfortable Space: Look for a peaceful, distraction-free environment. To make it more comfortable, add pillows, dim the lights, or use calming scents such as essential oils.

Choose a Guided Meditation: Investigate many guided meditation formats to see which one best meets your needs. You might choose those that focus on mindfulness, relaxation, or visions for specific objectives.

Maintain an Open Mind: Put your biases aside and simply allow yourself to experience the meditation. Naturally, thoughts will emerge. Accept them and gradually shift your concentration back to the guide's voice or the current exercise.

Allow yourself time to ponder on your thoughts and observations after each session. Consistent journaling of your experiences can enhance the advantages of meditation.

By including guided meditations into your daily routine, you can strengthen your mindfulness practice and create a tranquil haven in the midst of chaos.

6. Methods of affirmation and visualization

The capacity to see

Visualization, which conjures up vivid images in your mind, is a powerful mental tool that can help you relax, perform better, and achieve your goals. Mental practice can help you train your body and mind to respond favorably to real-life events.

Studies show that visualizing can increase physical performance, reduce anxiety, and boost self-confidence. Athletes frequently utilize visualization techniques to psychologically prepare for tournaments, envisioning themselves winning their events. This talent can help you feel better and manage stress more effectively.

Creating Strong Proclamations

Affirmations are positive comments that boost confidence and promote positivity. They act as a gentle reminder of your abilities and characteristics, helping to eliminate any negative thoughts that may occur under duress.

How to Create Effective Affirmations.

Be Specific: Create clear, concise affirmations aimed at your goals. Make the remark, "I am confidently presenting my ideas in front of my colleagues," rather than simply saying, "I am successful."

Using the present tense to frame affirmations makes them appear true. This strategy helps to shape your thinking, giving you confidence in your talents.

Keep It Positive: Try to focus on the good things that will happen rather than the bad. Say, "I am prepared and capable of succeeding," rather than, "I won't fail."

Personalize it: Write affirmations that are relevant to your goals and life experiences. The more meaningful things are to you, the greater their impact will be.

Repeat Frequently: Work affirmations into your everyday routine. You can recite them in front of a mirror, record them in a journal, or say them while meditating.

Procedures for Maintaining Daily Confidence.

Morning Routines: Affirmations might help you start the day off on a positive note. Take a deep breath, stand in front of the mirror, and repeat your affirmations aloud.

Exercises for Visualization: Set aside some time to imagine your goals and dreams. Imagine yourself completing them correctly and clearly. Feel the emotions that come with success.

Keeping a Gratitude Journal: Each day, make a list of three things for which you are grateful in your gratitude notebook. Focusing on the positive aspects of your life increases resilience and self-esteem.

To put your aspirations on paper, create a vision board that depicts them. Fill it with inspirational quotations and photos to serve as a constant reminder of your goals.

Reminders for Mindfulness: Take regular breaks during the day to breathe, ponder, and recognize your true potential. Use your breath as an anchor to help you concentrate and return to a state of calm.

By including visualization and affirmation activities into your daily routine, you may create a strong and confident attitude that will allow you to face obstacles head on.

Section III: Building Self-Belief in Difficult Situations.

There are several situations in life that might make us feel vulnerable and lose confidence. Building confidence is vital for negotiating difficult conversations, unexpected difficulties, and high-pressure situations successfully. This section of the book provides practical advice on how to prepare, communicate effectively, and develop emotional intelligence so that you can deal with tough situations with grace and confidence.

7. Planning and preparing

The Advantages of Forward Planning

Being ready is the foundation of confidence. When we plan ahead of time and foresee probable obstacles, we are better able to respond effectively rather than rashly. Preparedness not only reduces anxiety, but it also gives us a sense of control in unexpected situations.

Remember a time when you conquered a challenging situation. It could have been a job interview, a challenging chat with a loved one, or a professional presentation. How did preparation impact your performance? Research regularly reveals that those who put out the time to prepare are more likely to feel competent and achieve their goals. In this section, we'll discuss the significance of preparation and offer you with the resources you need to lay a firm foundation for success.

Developing Action Plans for Common Situations

An action plan serves as a road map, allowing you to successfully and effectively navigate difficult situations. Outlining specific activities reduces ambiguity and improves your ability to overcome hurdles. Use these tactics to construct successful action plans for common events:

Identify the Challenge: Before you begin, make sure you understand the scenario you wish to address. Is it a difficult conversation, a challenging task, or a public speech? Understanding the problem will make it easier to devise focused solutions.

Set specific objectives: What are your goals? Set specific, attainable goals to guide your efforts. For example, if you're preparing for a presentation, your goal could be to keep the audience's attention and communicate your point clearly.

Steps to Success Outline: Divide your goals into small chunks. Determine the steps required to attain each goal. For example, if you're prepared for a difficult conversation, you might do:

Looking at the topic or issue.

Choose your major concepts.

Grace Under Pressure

Say what you want to say again.

Deal with challenges: Consider probable roadblocks. How will you handle them? Being prepared for challenges allows you to tackle them elegantly and calmly.

Practice Your Plan: By implementing your action plan, you will feel more at ease and confident. Practicing allows you to refine your plan and identify areas for improvement.

Think and Adjust: After implementing your plan, consider what worked and what didn't. What worked best? What can be improved? Use this information to alter your strategy for future incidents.

Developing action plans based on typical scenarios will help you confront difficulties with clarity and forcefulness.

Having tough talks when playing

Role-playing is an effective way to prepare for uncomfortable interactions. Simulating real-life scenarios allows you to enhance your communication skills, gain a better understanding of your emotions, and practice responding.

How to Engage in Effective Role Playing:

Choose a Partner: Look for someone trustworthy to role-play with. This could be a friend, family member, or colleague who is prepared to give constructive comments.

Create the Scenario: Clearly describe the discussion you wish to practice. Provide clear details about the situation, the people involved, and the main topics you wish to discuss.

Take turns speaking and representing the opposite side or the listener. This technique helps both participants develop empathy and perspective-taking skills.

Pay attention to your tone, body language, and clarity of expression while role-playing. Allow your companion enough space to completely articulate their opinions in order to learn active listening.

Request Feedback: After each role-playing exercise, describe what worked well and what could have been improved. Constructive feedback helps people gain confidence and improve their technique.

Repeat the scenario, making any necessary alterations based on the audience's response. As you practice more, your confidence will increase.

Role-playing challenging conversations helps you improve your communication skills and prepare for real-life scenarios. This will help you express yourself effectively in difficult situations.

8. Communication Proficiency

'Ability to Pay Close Attention

Effective communication includes both speaking and listening. To actively listen, one must focus completely on the speaker, grasp what they are saying, and react wisely. Honest conversation is promoted in a setting that promotes respect and compassion via active listening.

Key Aspects of Intentional Listening:

Be Aware: Give the speaker your full attention. Set aside your distractions, make eye contact, and demonstrate that you are there.

Show That You Understand: Use both spoken and nonverbal signs to indicate that you are paying attention. We encourage the speaker to continue by nodding, keeping an open posture, and saying things like "I see" or "I understand."

Think and Explain: Summarize or paraphrase the speaker's remarks to ensure you comprehend what they are saying. "So what I hear you saying is..."

encourages the speaker to elaborate while also assuring them that you understand.

Avoid interrupting: Wait until the other person has finished speaking before responding. Let them finish their ideas before reacting.

Ask Open-Ended inquiries: Open-ended inquiries can spark a deeper conversation. This method encourages the speaker to provide more information about their thoughts and feelings.

Active listening improves communication skills and fosters better relationships, all of which are required for managing difficult situations gracefully.

How to Speak Calmly and Clear

Even in challenging situations, successful communication requires clarity, calm, and confidence. The following tips will help you become a better communicator:

Stay grounded: Before you speak, take a moment to gather your thoughts. Inhale deeply, focus on your message, and bring your thoughts back to a center.

Use "I" statements to focus your remarks on your own feelings and thoughts rather than criticizing or accusing others. Say "I feel overwhelmed when deadlines are tight," rather than "You always put me under pressure."

Be Brief and Clear: Avoid jargon and talk clearly. Aim for clarity to make sure your message is comprehended.

Maintain Calm: What you say has a significant impact on how others see you. Even if the conversation becomes heated, maintain your calm and communicate properly.

Manage Your Body Language: Communication is influenced equally by spoken and nonverbal cues. Maintain an open, relaxed posture while stressing your remarks with non-aggressive motions.

When communicating, try to understand the other person's point of view. Empathy allows you to understand their sentiments and make more informed decisions.

If you're feeling emotional, take a moment to collect your thoughts. A little period of silence can help you avoid misinterpretation and provide yourself time to ponder your response.

By using these tactics, you may confidently express yourself even in tough situations, allowing you to communicate more effectively and reduce conflict.

Handling Conflict with Grace.

Life will undoubtedly entail conflict, but how you handle it can have a significant impact on your relationships and sense of self. Managing disagreements with elegance necessitates remaining calm and respectful even in stressful times. The tactics suggested below will help you deal with disagreement productively.

Keep Your Cool: When confronted with a quarrel, pause and take a few deep breaths. When you maintain your composure, you may think more clearly and behave rationally rather than emotionally.

Maintain Focus on the Issue: Instead of bringing up personal complaints or assigning blame, keep the discussion on the current topic. This technique promotes fruitful communication and problem solving.

Recognize Differences: It is common to have different points of view. Recognize and respect the feelings of others, even if you disagree with their point of view.

Collaborate to Find Solutions: Look at dispute as a chance for collaboration. Work together to find practical solutions that fulfill everyone's needs. This type of thinking promotes collaboration rather than competition.

Know When to Leave: If the conversation becomes too heated or irrelevant, it is appropriate to end it. Encourage a courteous break and return to the matter later, when the stress has subsided.

After a disagreement has been resolved, follow up by contacting the other party. By checking in again, you demonstrate your commitment to the partnership and assist to avoid future misunderstandings.

When you handle conflict gracefully, you may maintain your composure, improve connections, and emerge from challenging situations with confidence.

9. How Emotional Intelligence Develops.

Acknowledging your emotions

Emotional intelligence (EI) refers to the ability to perceive, analyze, and control emotions in oneself and others. Developing emotional intelligence allows you to handle challenging situations with grace and compassion.

Key Characteristics of Emotional Intelligence:

Self-awareness: Recognizing your own feelings is the first step toward emotional intelligence. Think about your emotions, reactions, and triggers on a regular basis. Keeping a journal may help you identify your emotional tendencies.

Self-Regulation: Once you've become aware of your emotions, work on your self-regulation skills. This entails controlling your emotions, particularly when circumstances are challenging. You can keep control by using strategies such as mindfulness, deep breathing, and taking breaks.

Motivation: Aligning your goals with your values will help you develop intrinsic motivation. Understanding what motivates you allows you to remain tough and focused under hardship.

Social Awareness: Develop empathy by recognizing other people's feelings. This skill improves your ability to connect with others and respond sympathetically in challenging situations.

Relationship management requires two key components: dispute resolution and effective communication. Building strong relationships necessitates collaboration, gratitude, and active listening.

Increasing your emotional intelligence can help you be more resilient in challenging situations, form lasting connections, and handle life's challenges with courage and self-assurance.

The Use of Empathy in Difficult Situations

Empathy is the foundation of emotional intelligence since it allows for more meaningful connections with others. In tough situations, empathy training can help to build understanding and change conflict into cooperation. This is how empathy develops:

Participate in Active Listening: As previously said, active listening is an essential component of empathy. Giving someone your complete attention is one way to show that you respect their opinions and feelings.

Try to put yourself in their shoes and see things from their perspective. Consider their possible feelings and the factors that impact them. This exercise promotes understanding and empathy.

Validate Their Feelings: You should appreciate someone else's feelings, even if you disagree with them. Saying something like, "I know this is very important to you," demonstrates that you care about their sentiments.

React Compassionately: Instead of passing judgment on someone else's feelings, respond with compassion. To create a safe environment for candid discussion, demonstrate compassion and support.

Consider Your Own Feelings: Being aware of your own emotions may help you relate more effectively with others. By recreating your emotions, you can compare your experiences to those of others.

Empathy is crucial in building trust and resolving disagreements. By honing this skill, you can handle challenging situations with grace and form important connections with people.

Methods for Regulating Emotions

While emotions are a normal aspect of being human, controlling them is critical for retaining composure and self-assurance under pressure. You can improve your emotional regulation by using the following practical techniques:

If you're feeling overwhelmed, take a moment to pause and breathe deeply. Deep breathing may help you regain your composure by activating the body's relaxation response.

Identify Triggers: Consider the situations that elicit powerful emotional responses. Knowing your triggers allows you to predict and control your reactions.

Practice mindfulness: By focusing on the present moment, you can develop a judgment-free awareness of your emotions. Regular mindfulness practice helps you respond consciously rather than involuntarily.

Reframe Negative ideas: When faced with a challenging situation, resist the want to have negative or destructive ideas. Reframing is the practice of replacing negative ideas with constructive ones.

Develop self-compassion by treating yourself with love and understanding, especially when faced with a

Grace Under Pressure

difficult situation. Recognize that you are trying your best and that having feelings is natural.

Seek Help: If you're having trouble controlling your emotions, talk to a friend, family member, or a mental health professional. Talking about your emotions can help you get perspective and feel less overwhelmed.

You may boost your resilience and confidence in stressful situations by employing these techniques to better control your emotional reactions.

Section IV: Demonstrating Empathy during Stress

The capacity to retain cool under duress in a world that can appear chaotic and overwhelming is a valuable skill to develop. Events that test our ability to recover, such as an important presentation, a family crisis, or an unexpected setback, might help to highlight our strengths. This section will examine common scenarios that put people under strain, highlight the triumphs of those who confronted these obstacles head on, and provide realistic techniques for long-term resilience building in a caring atmosphere.

10. Case Studies and Actual Situations

Typical Situations That Increase Stress

Knowing the common conditions that cause pressure allows you to better prepare for and manage these situations. Here are some situations that many individuals get into:

Public Speaking: Being in front of an audience may be stressful for anyone, regardless of experience level. Even the most experienced presenters can become paralyzed by the fear of misinterpreting, making a mistake, or missing something important.

Job interviews: The pressure to impress potential employers might lead to increased anxiety levels. Many applicants are concerned about their credentials and reputation.

Family Conflicts: Tensions can rise and cause high emotions during gatherings or conflicts. Managing sensitive issues can be difficult, especially when emotions are high.

Crisis Situations: Unexpected events, such as accidents or natural disasters, can produce worry and confusion. Rapid thought and poise in the face of chaos are required for an effective response.

Life Transitions: Moving to a new location, changing careers, or getting divorced can all cause major stress.

Success Stories: How a Few Were Able to Maintain their Cool

Case Study 1: The Fearless Speaker

Emily, a marketing executive, was forced to confront her biggest fears when she was invited to speak at a global conference. Despite her competence, she felt nervous to appear in front of powerful industry executives. Instead of surrendering to dread, Emily used numerous tactics to keep her cool:

Emily prepared by practicing her speech and familiarizing herself with the issue. She felt more confident now that she was prepared.

She pictured herself succeeding and earning praise, which helped to calm her nerves.

Breathing Techniques: Emily used deep breathing to calm herself down before hitting the stage for her presentation.

Emily received appreciation for her observations, and her presentation went well. She turned her fear into a strong performance by rehearsing and visualizing it.

Study 2: The Silent Interviewee.

Political disagreements erupted during a family gathering. Because of his calm manner, Alex decided to intervene. He chose to extinguish the flames rather than fanning them higher.

Active Listening: Alex listened to the other person's feelings without offering his own. This made everyone feel valued and heard.

Empathy: By sharing a personal tale relevant to the topic, he humanized the discussion and reinforced everyone's shared ideals.

Redirecting the Conversation: After calming the tension, Alex returned the conversation to a lighter topic.

Alex's plan did more than just diffuse the crisis; it also improved family relationships. Under duress, his ability to maintain cool and empathy demonstrated the value of emotional intelligence.

Lessons from high-stress situations

Planning is the key to reducing concern. This includes practicing a speech as well as planning for family dynamics.

Empathy and active listening: Understanding other people's viewpoints helps to build rapport and reduce conflict.

A.T Ramos

Breathe and stay grounded: Deep breathing might help you regain control and make sensible judgments during panic attacks.

Focus on Solutions: To promote resilience and peace of mind, shift your perspective from problem-centered to solution-oriented.

By learning about these tactics and success stories, readers can enhance their capacity to deal with pressure gracefully, which they can then implement in their own lives.

11. Developing a Network of Assistance

How Support Systems Work:

Having a strong support network can be quite valuable during difficult times. Support networks can provide people with emotional, practical, and social support as they manage with stress. The importance of support systems is as follows.

Emotional Support: Friends and relatives can provide a sympathetic ear and offer emotional support during difficult times, reducing feelings of loneliness.

A support system can help with practical problems like allocating duties or providing relaxing aids.

Perspective and counsel: Trustworthy friends or mentors can provide new viewpoints and counsel, allowing people to make difficult decisions while remaining calm under pressure.

Forming Your Own Organization

Creating a friendly workplace demands intentionally cultivating your own tribe of like-minded folks. Take the following steps to build a strong support system:

Assess Your Needs: Consider the type of support you require, whether emotional, practical, or both. Understanding your requirements will guide your hiring decisions.

Reach Out: Strike up a conversation with friends, relatives, or colleagues. Inform them that you appreciate their support and would like to remain in touch.

Engage in the Community: Join local groups or clubs that cater to your interests. This broadens your social circle and links you with others who share your values and inspire you.

Build Relationships: Spend effort making and maintaining contacts. This could include simply being present for one another, keeping up with things on a regular basis, or participating in activities together.

Support Mutually: Give your allies your complete attention. Building a link for mutual benefit strengthens ties and fosters trust.

Obtaining Professional Help When Needed

While friends and family can be great sources of support, there may be times when professional help is required. When should you consider obtaining specialist mental health care?

Persistent Stress or Anxiety: If stress or anxiety persists despite self-help efforts or interferes with everyday tasks, a therapist can provide helpful skills and strategies.

Trauma or Crisis: A traumatic incident might elicit intense emotions. While the healing process is ongoing, you might seek assistance from an expert.

Relationship issues: By creating a secure environment for open discussion, family or couples therapy can help to resolve conflicts and develop bonds between partners.

Self-Exploration: Counseling can help you improve your emotional intelligence and resilience while also serving as an important instrument for personal growth and discovery.

Remember that seeking professional guidance is an indication of strength. It reflects your dedication to your own development and well-being.

12. Long-Term Strategies for Maintaining Calm

Create a Personal Resilience Plan.

A personal resilience plan outlines how resilience can be developed in everyday situations. Here's how to make one.

Consider Your Past Difficulties When Assessing Your Resilience. Examine your response and find any places where you may have performed better.

Set specific resilience goals, such as increasing coping abilities in difficult situations or enhancing emotional control.

Identify Resources: Make a list of resources, approaches, and support systems that can help you improve resilience. These could be motivational speakers, books, or seminars.

Create a Routine: Include resilience-boosting activities that take place on a regular basis. Journaling, exercising, or practicing meditation can all help you process your feelings.

Assess and Adjust: Evaluate your progress on a regular basis and adjust your plan as needed. Resilience is a dynamic process that evolves with time.

Daily Practices for Self-Care

If you want to stay resilient and calm, you must incorporate self-care activities into your daily routine. Here are some helpful self-care strategies:

Meditation and mindfulness: Mindfulness training reduces anxiety, improves emotional regulation, and promotes present moment awareness.

Physical Activity: Regular exercise boosts mood, releases endorphins, and improves overall health. Allow time for your hobbies and interests.

Grace Under Pressure

Good Nutrition: Eating a balanced diet promotes both physical and mental health. Feed your body nutritious foods to keep it nourished and energized.

Enough Sleep: To refresh your body and mind, make getting enough sleep a top priority. Create a calming environment and stick to a regular sleep schedule.

Writing, drawing, gardening, and other artistic pursuits provide excellent opportunities for self-expression and relaxation.

The importance of introspection and modification.

Regular reflection is essential for personal development and resilience. Here's how to develop a contemplative practice.

Daily Journaling: Set aside time each day to reflect on your thoughts and experiences from the past. Keeping a journal can assist discover behavioral patterns and facilitate the processing of emotions.

Weekly Check-Ins: Set aside some time every week to review your emotional condition and go over your resilience tactics. Do they work? What adjustments are feasible?

Adaptation: Your techniques may need to alter as a result of the ongoing changes in life. Stay adaptable and open to new notions that match your circumstances right now.

Celebrate Your Successes: No matter how modest, make sure to recognize and honor your accomplishments. This encourages continual growth and upholds moral behavior.

Take on Challenges: View setbacks as opportunities for progress. Reframe setbacks as useful learning experiences that enhance your resilience.

By employing these long-term tactics, you may create the resilience and calmness that will allow you to tackle life's obstacles with confidence and grace.

A.T Ramos

Concluding Remarks: Your Road to Perpetual Calm

As we manage the obstacles of modern life, maintaining our composure under duress is a crucial ability that can benefit our personal and professional lives. In this book, we've discussed a wide range of methods that might help you develop the emotional intelligence and resilience needed to handle life's obstacles with confidence and grace. Now that we've addressed the most critical tactics, let's go over them again and look forward to supporting you in obtaining lasting peace.

An overview of key methods

Breathing Techniques: First, we examined the science of breathing and how much it affects our mental health. Breathing techniques such as diaphragmatic breathing and the 4-7-8 deliver immediate peace and are great tools to add into your everyday routine. By focusing on your breath, you can ground yourself in the present moment, reducing tension and increasing calm.

Meditation and mindfulness: Mindfulness helps us cope with the stresses of daily life by encouraging the development of present-moment awareness. Simple mindfulness techniques and guided meditations can help you reconnect with your inner self while also increasing resilience and clarity. Developing these practices can improve your general health and change how you deal with stress.

Techniques for Creating Strong Affirmations and Using Images: We investigated affirmations' transformative potential as well as their ability to generate powerful imagery. Engaging in constructive self-talk and practicing successful visualization can help you gain confidence and prepare your mind to face obstacles with composure. Frequent visualization and affirmation exercises provide a solid foundation for confidence development.

Planning and preparation: The importance of organization cannot be emphasized. We talked about how you might feel more safe by practicing awkward encounters and developing plans of action for typical situations. Anticipating potential hurdles and finding solutions to overcome them prepares you to behave calmly and coolly under pressure.

Effective Communication Skills: The ability to listen carefully and express oneself calmly and effectively are two critical components of effective communication. Mastering the skill of elegant dispute resolution allows you to cultivate positive connections and create an environment that encourages open communication.

Gaining Emotional Intelligence: Recognizing your emotions and developing empathy are critical skills for dealing with challenging situations. We discussed how to manage your emotions so that you may respond carefully rather than impulsively.

Creating a Support System: As we examined how they may help you manage stress, it became evident how crucial it is to have a network of friends, family, and experts by your side. Building your own support network and seeking expert help when necessary can be quite valuable during challenging times.

Long-Term Strategies for Maintaining Calm: Finally, we discussed the need of creating a personal resilience plan, taking care of oneself, and being open to reflection and growth. These long-term techniques can assist you in developing resilience as a lifetime process that allows you to adjust to life's ever-changing challenges.

Taking on Challenges with Self-belief

With these tactics in your repertoire, you may be able to approach obstacles with newfound confidence. Life will always present challenges, but how you handle them will determine your experience. Change your viewpoint so that setbacks are viewed as opportunities for growth rather than insurmountable hurdles.

Whenever you are presented with a difficult work or an environment with heightened pressure, remind yourself of the strategies you have learned. Use your breathing techniques to ground yourself, imagine your success, and get inspiration from your support network. Remember that confidence is not the absence of fear, but rather the ability to move on in the face of it. By tackling obstacles head on, you build resilience and make it simpler to overcome them later.

It is not a race, but rather an ongoing progressive process that leads to serenity. You will have both victories and setbacks along the way, but every step you take toward mastering the art of remaining calm under pressure is a victory in and of itself. Celebrate your wins, no matter how minor, and recognize the fortitude required to face life's challenges.

Your Path To Lasting Serenity

As you begin your path, keep in mind that attaining enduring serenity is a unique and transforming experience. Each person's route to serenity is unique, influenced by their experiences, values, and goals. Here are some final considerations to help you get started:

Practice Frequently: Establishing new habits requires consistency. Make time every day to practice breathing exercises, visualization techniques, and mindfulness. The more you use these techniques, the more automatic they become.

Consider and Adjust: By reviewing and analyzing your experiences on a regular basis, you can determine what works best for you. Adjust your strategy as needed, and don't be hesitant to try something new. Getting out of your comfort zone is frequently the first step toward personal growth.

Grace Under Pressure

Stay Inquisitive: Approach obstacles with curiosity rather than fear. Recognize that hardships always teach us something, and keep an open mind about them. Thinking in this way promotes resilience and proactive problem resolution.

Build Relationships: Your support network is an invaluable resource. Spending time with folks that motivate and inspire you will help you build stronger relationships. Encourage free conversation and create a supportive community environment.

Give yourself sufficient attention. Taking care of oneself is essential for preserving balance and overall wellness. Make self-care a priority in your everyday routine. Prioritize hobbies, exercise, and relaxation—activities that lift your mood and give you new energy.

Accept Imperfection: Recognize that no one is flawless and that mistakes will always occur. Consider aiming for advancement rather than perfection. Be kind with yourself and give yourself space to grow and change.

Finally, take some time to respect and enjoy your peace journey. Recognize your accomplishments and successes. Gratitude for all experiences—good and bad—can help you gain a better understanding of your resilience and strength.

Finally, remember that learning to be graceful under pressure is a lifetime process that requires fortitude, forbearance, and a dedication to personal growth. Carry the knowledge and skills you gained from this book with you as you go forward. Face problems with open arms in order to achieve inner serenity each day. Even if the journey is difficult, maintaining resilience and calmness offers truly life-changing benefits.

Every decision you take has an impact on those around you and on your own life. When you are gracious in the midst of adversity, you set an example for others, encouraging them to approach their issues with confidence and composure. Let us go together

A.T Ramos

down this route to long-term peace, supporting one another.

The end

A.T Ramos

Grace Under Pressure

Printed in Great Britain
by Amazon